I0409365

This coloring book

belongs to:

....

....

....

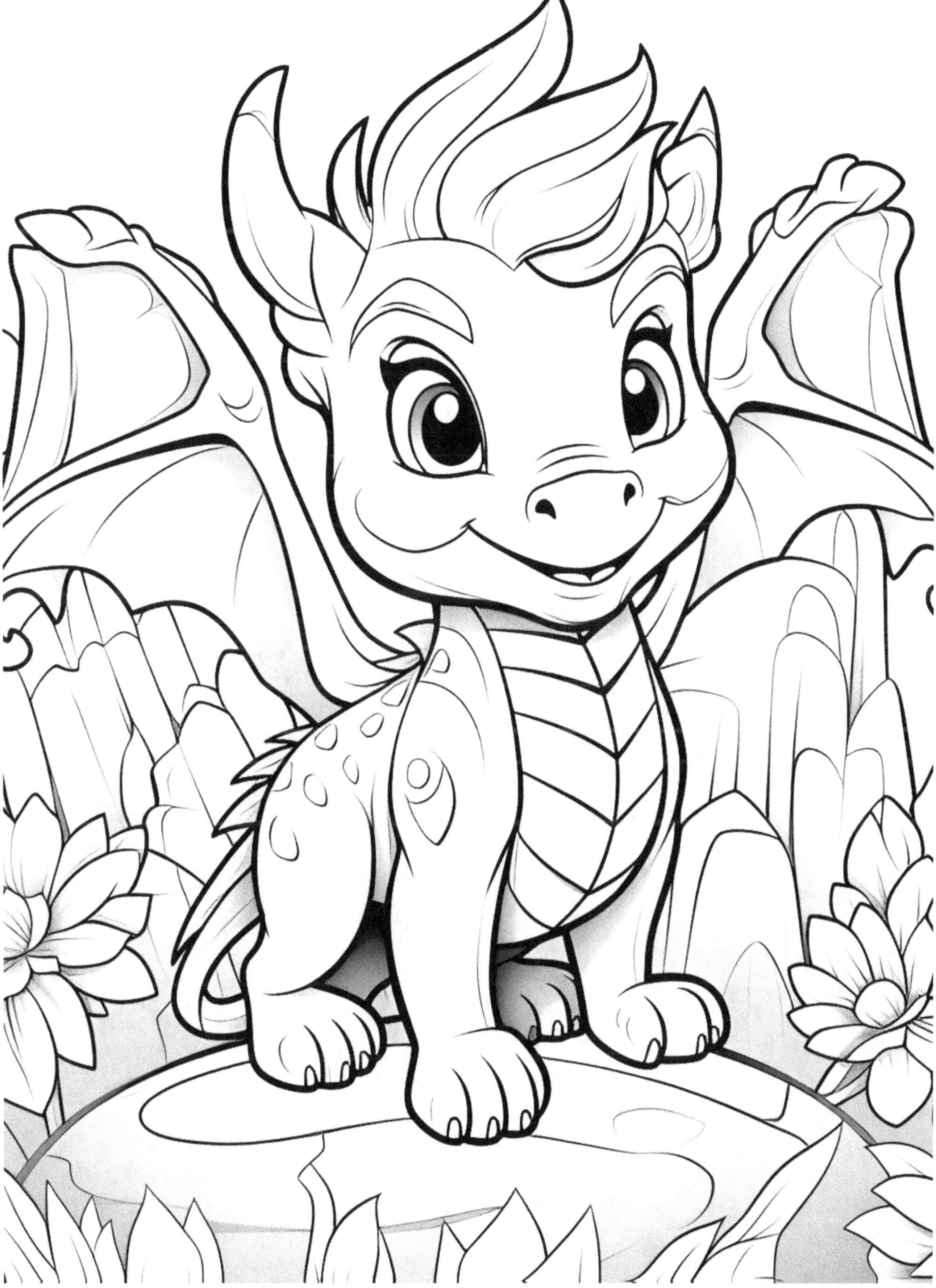

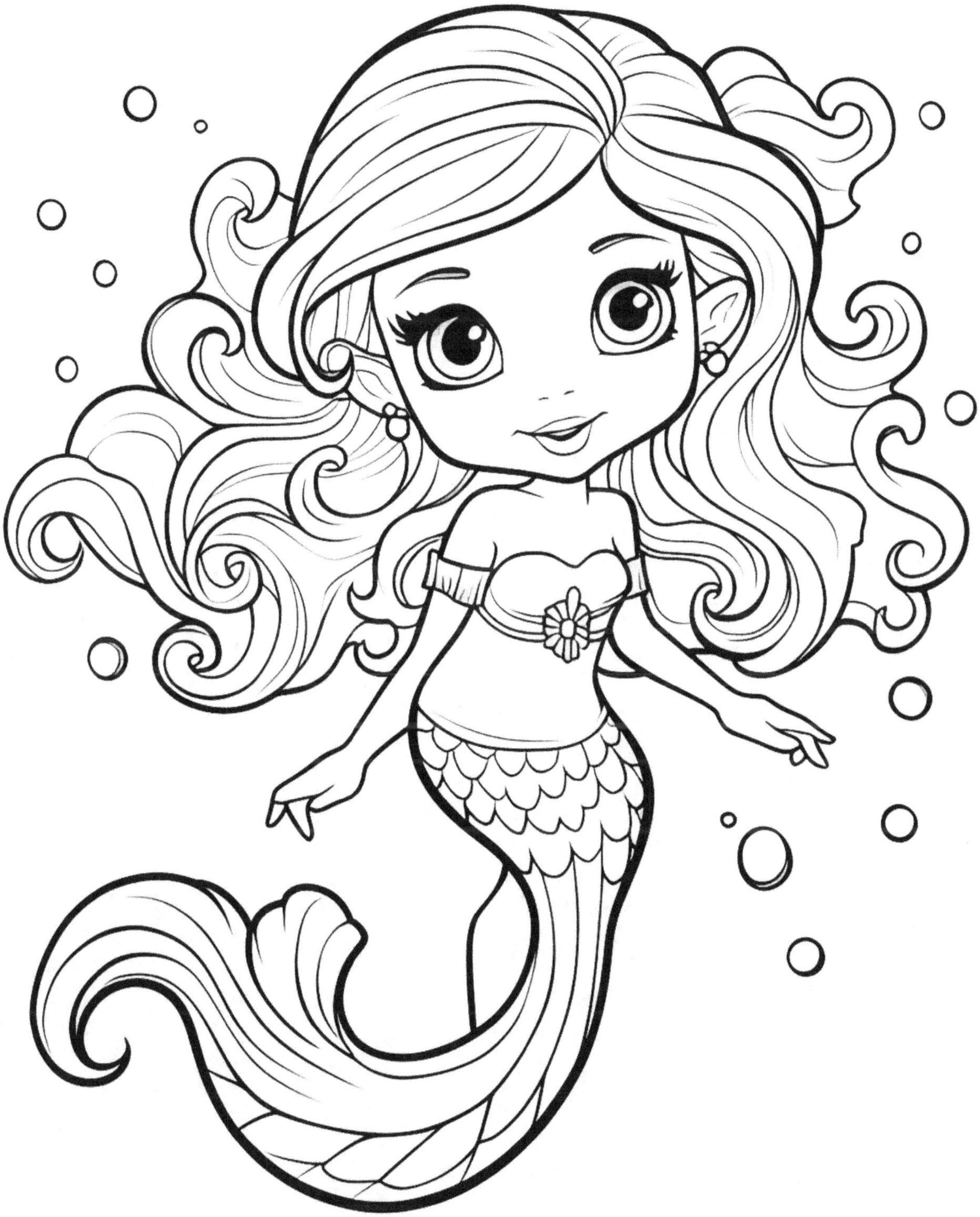

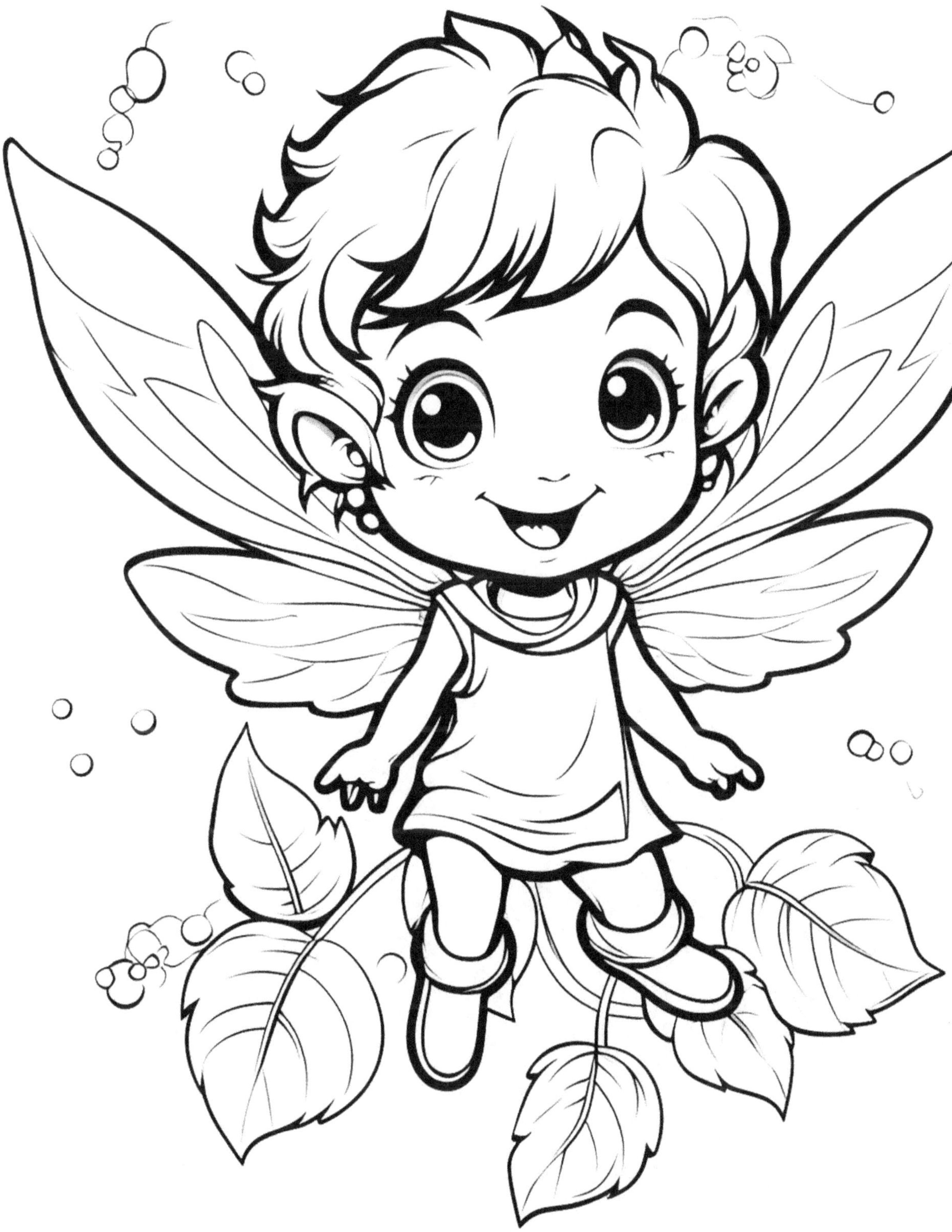

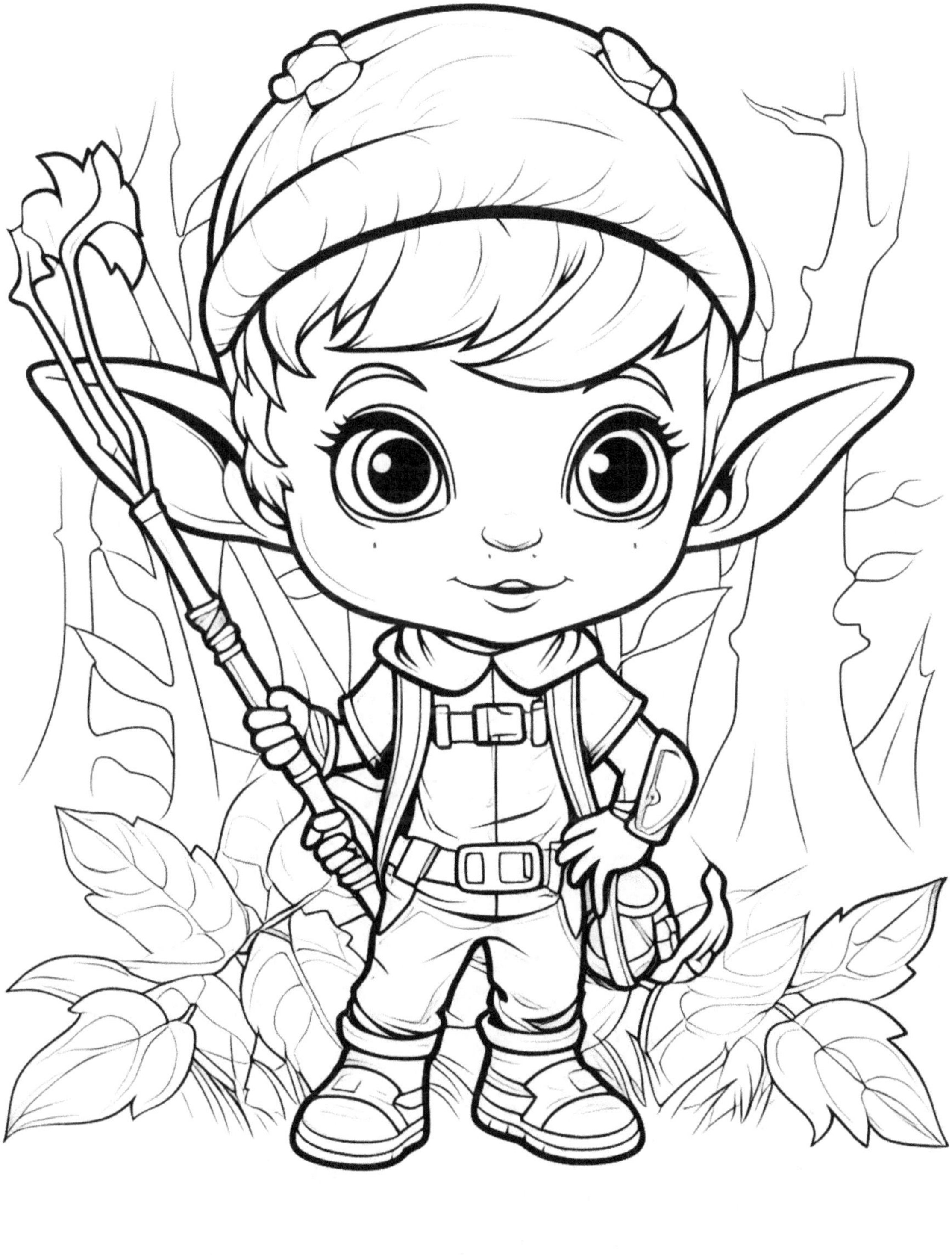

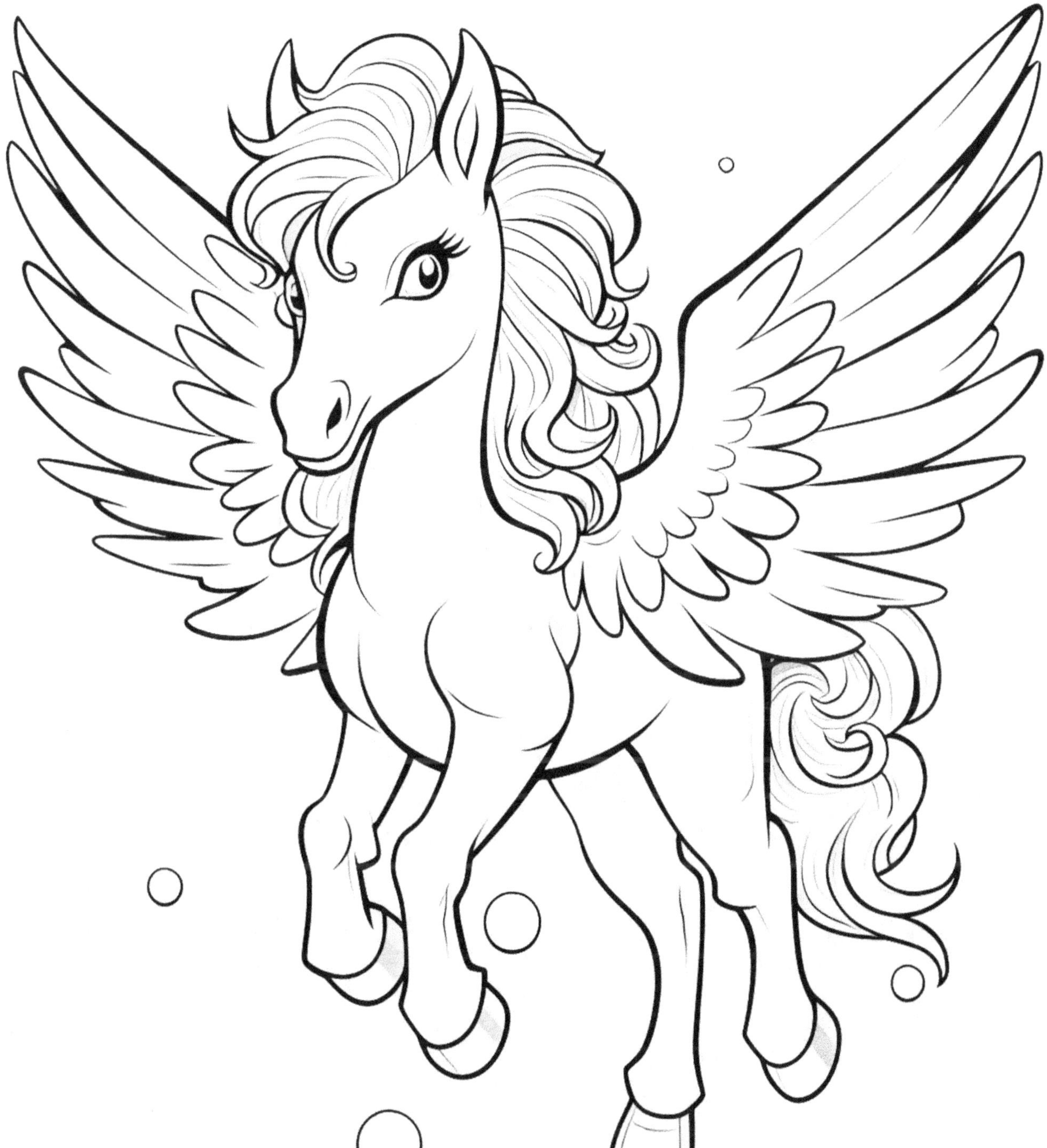

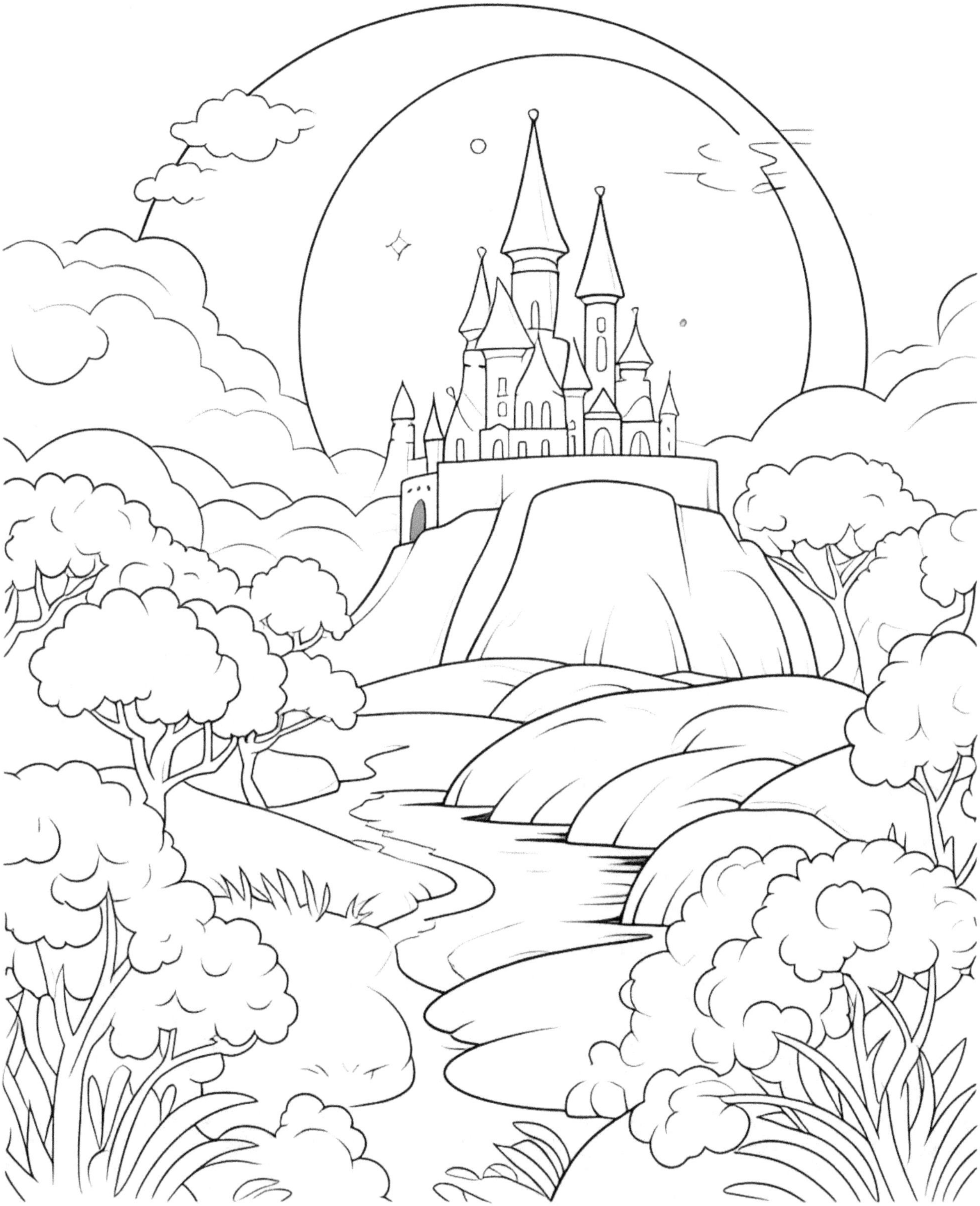

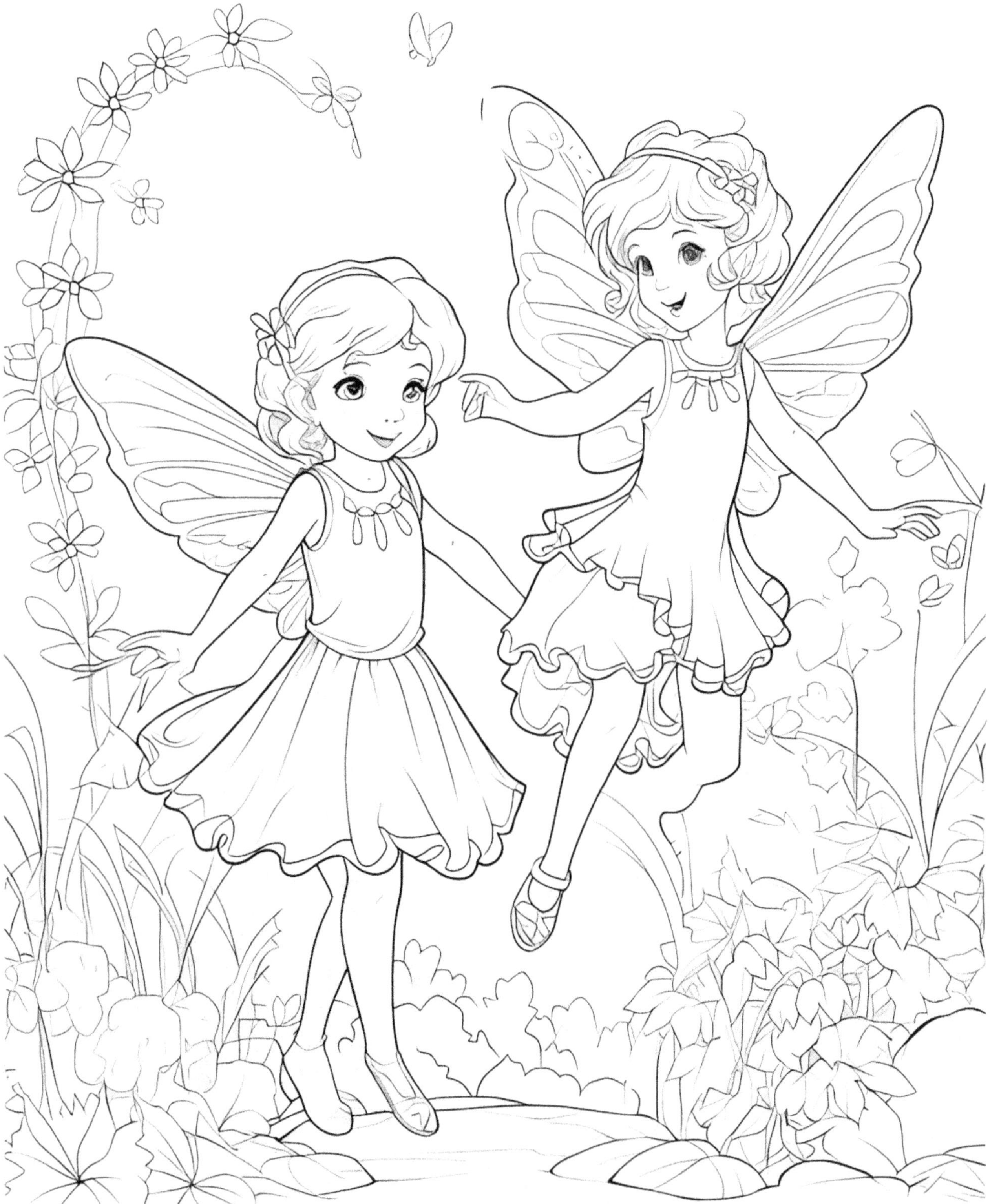

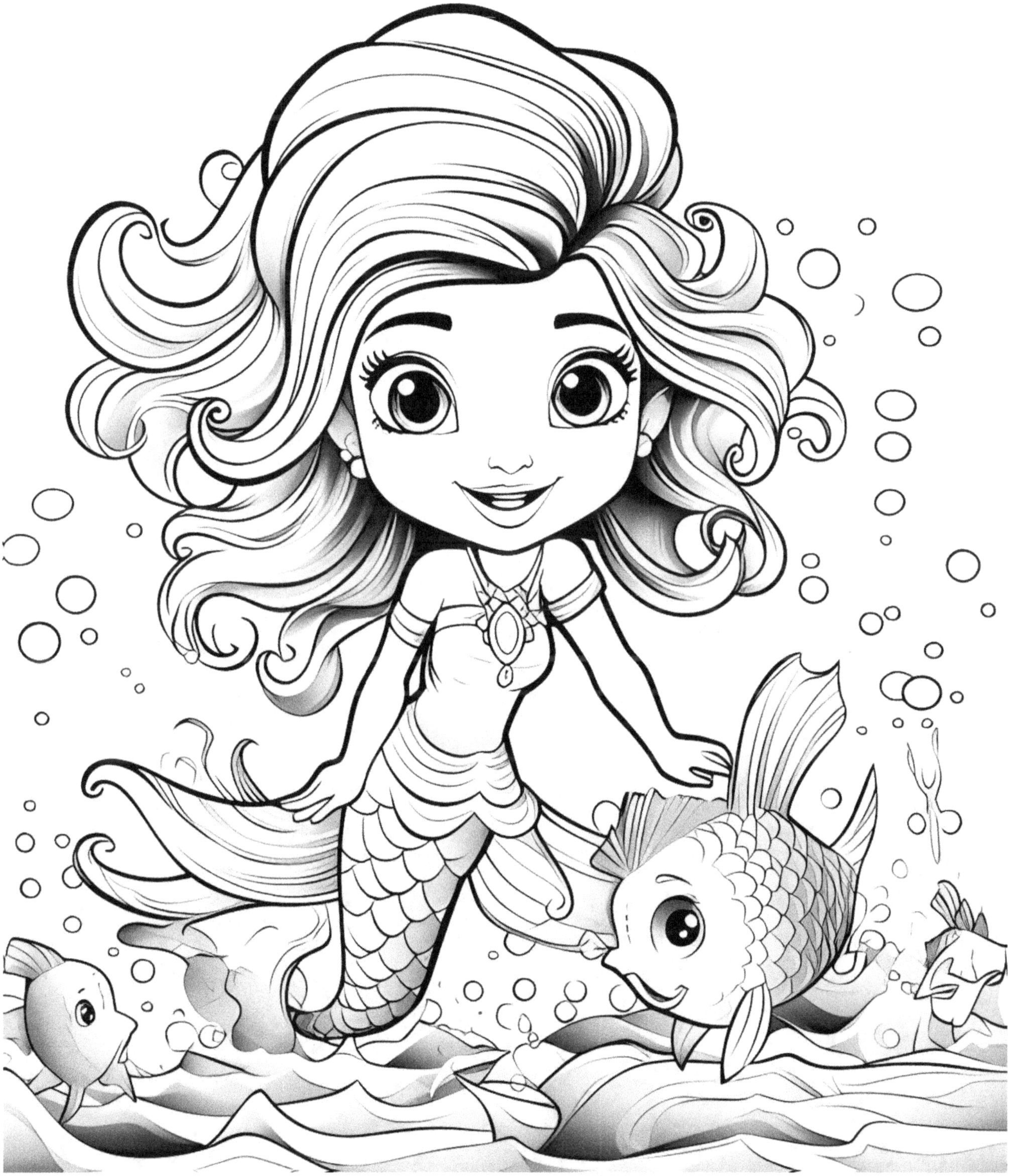

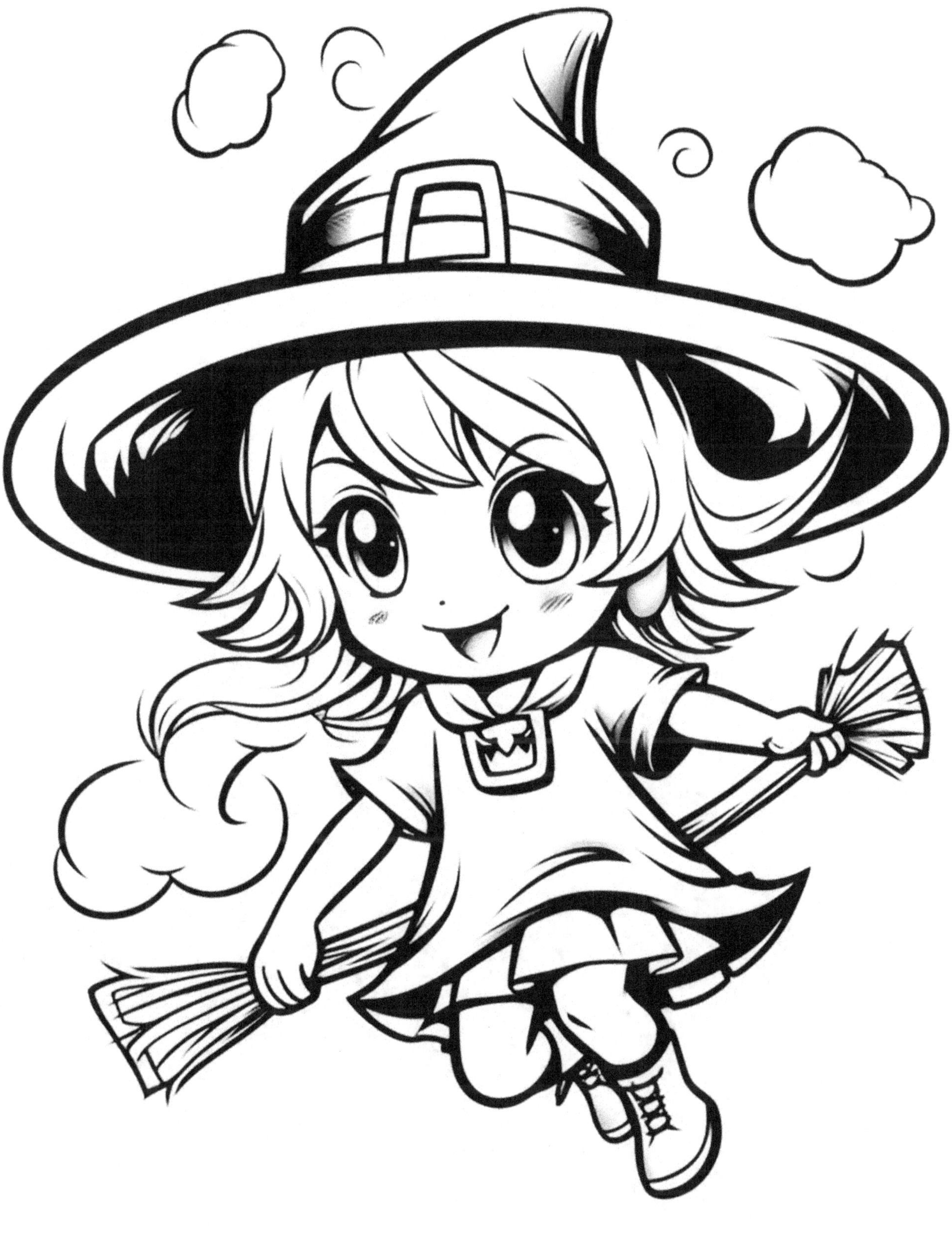

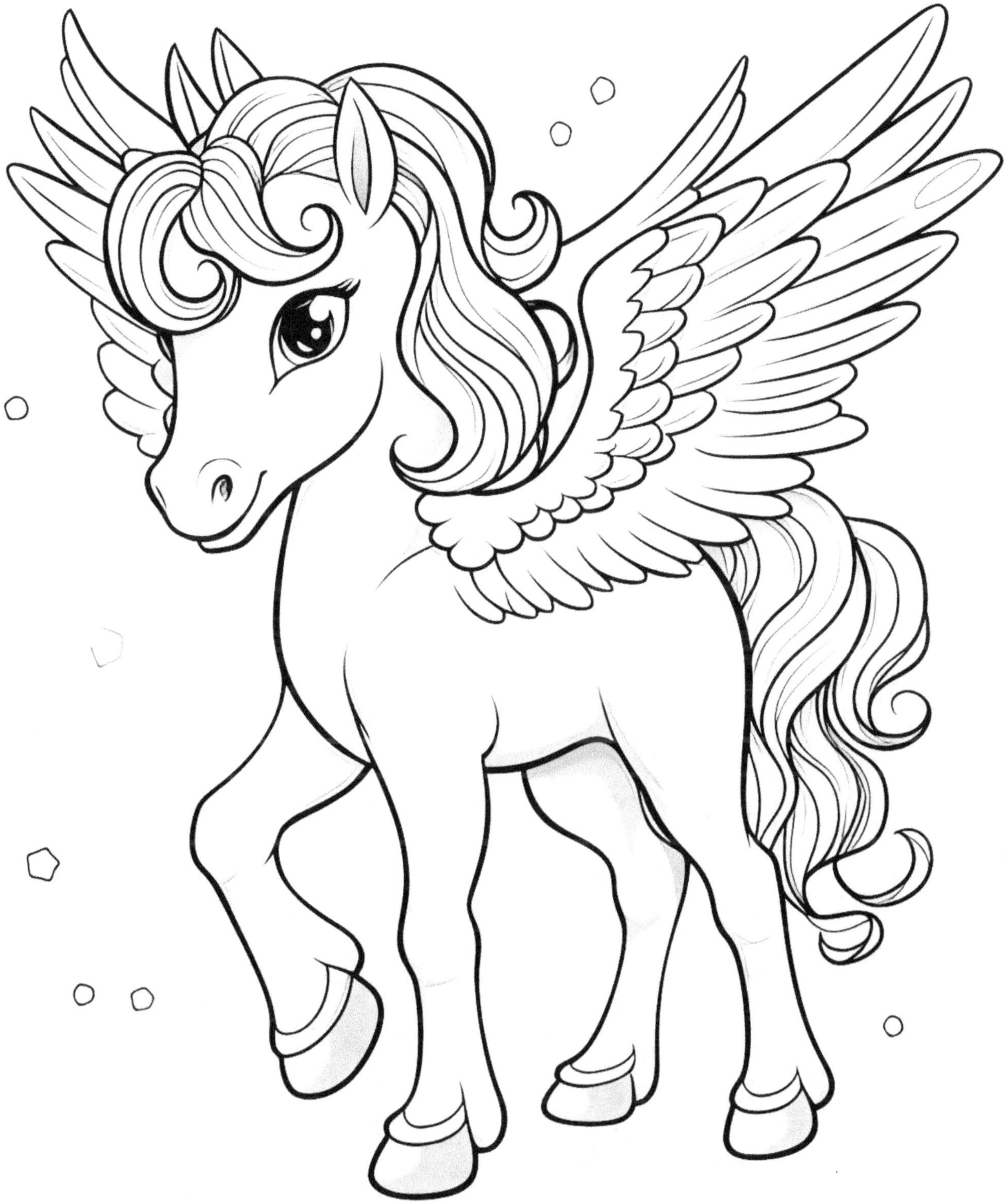

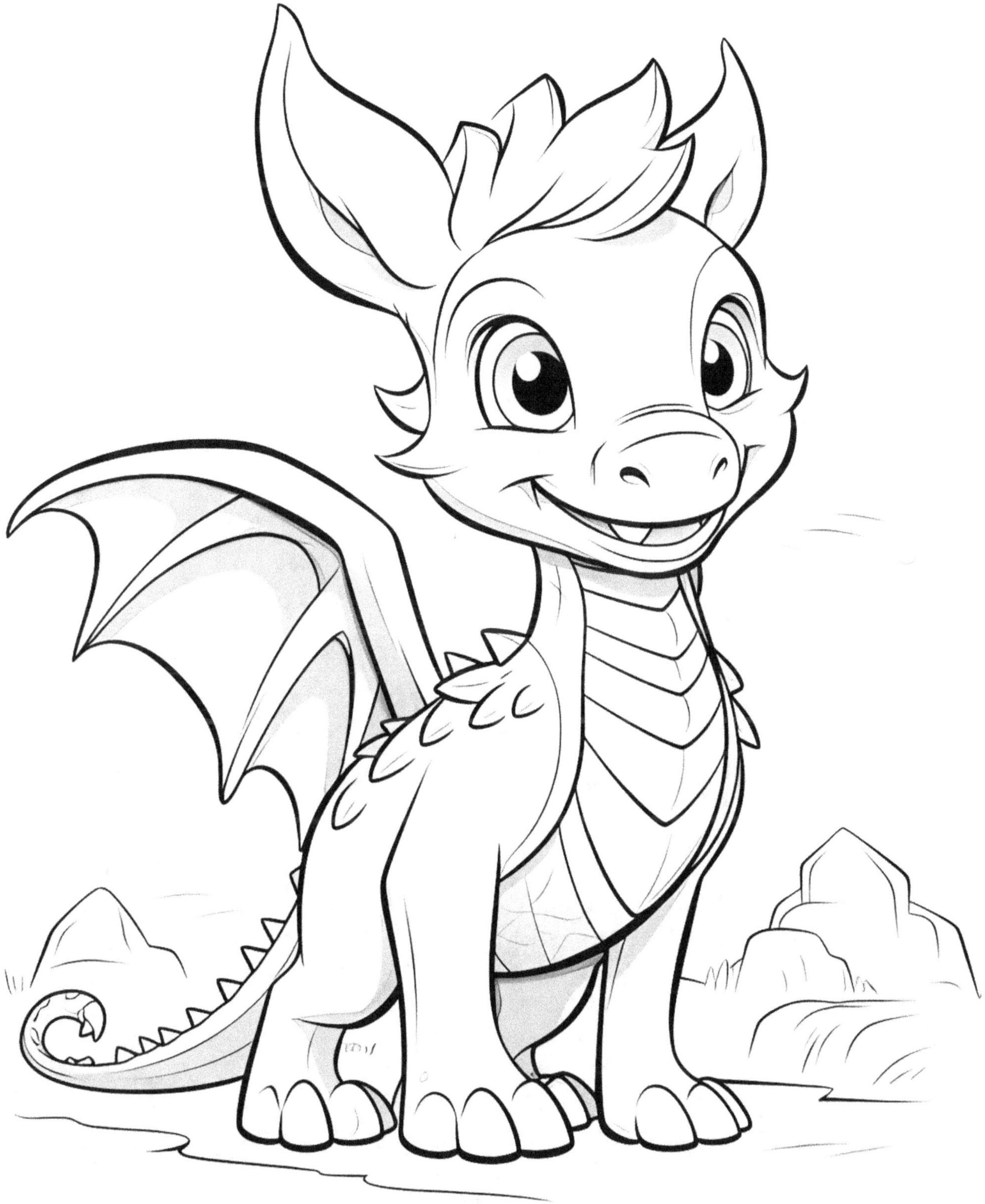

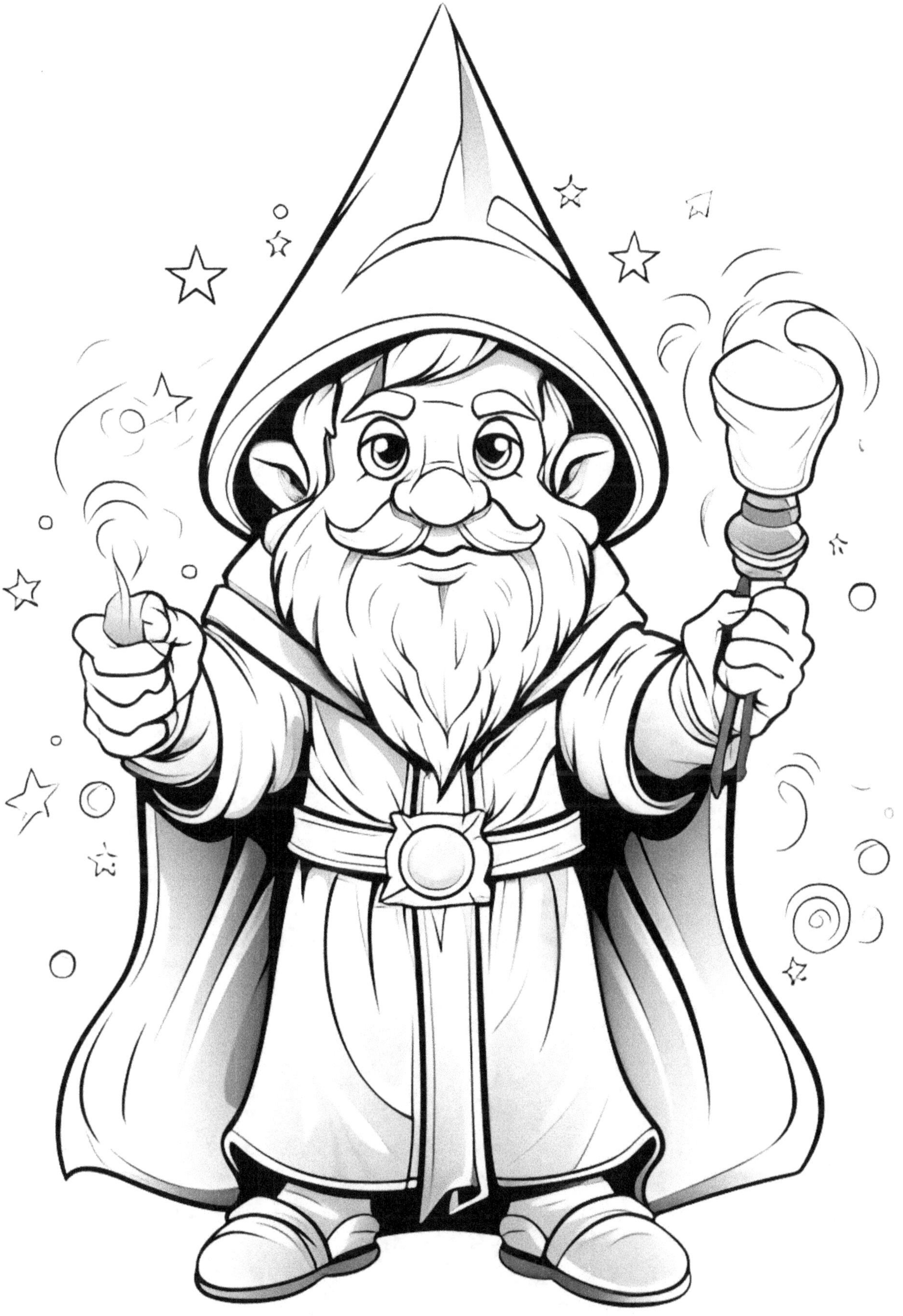

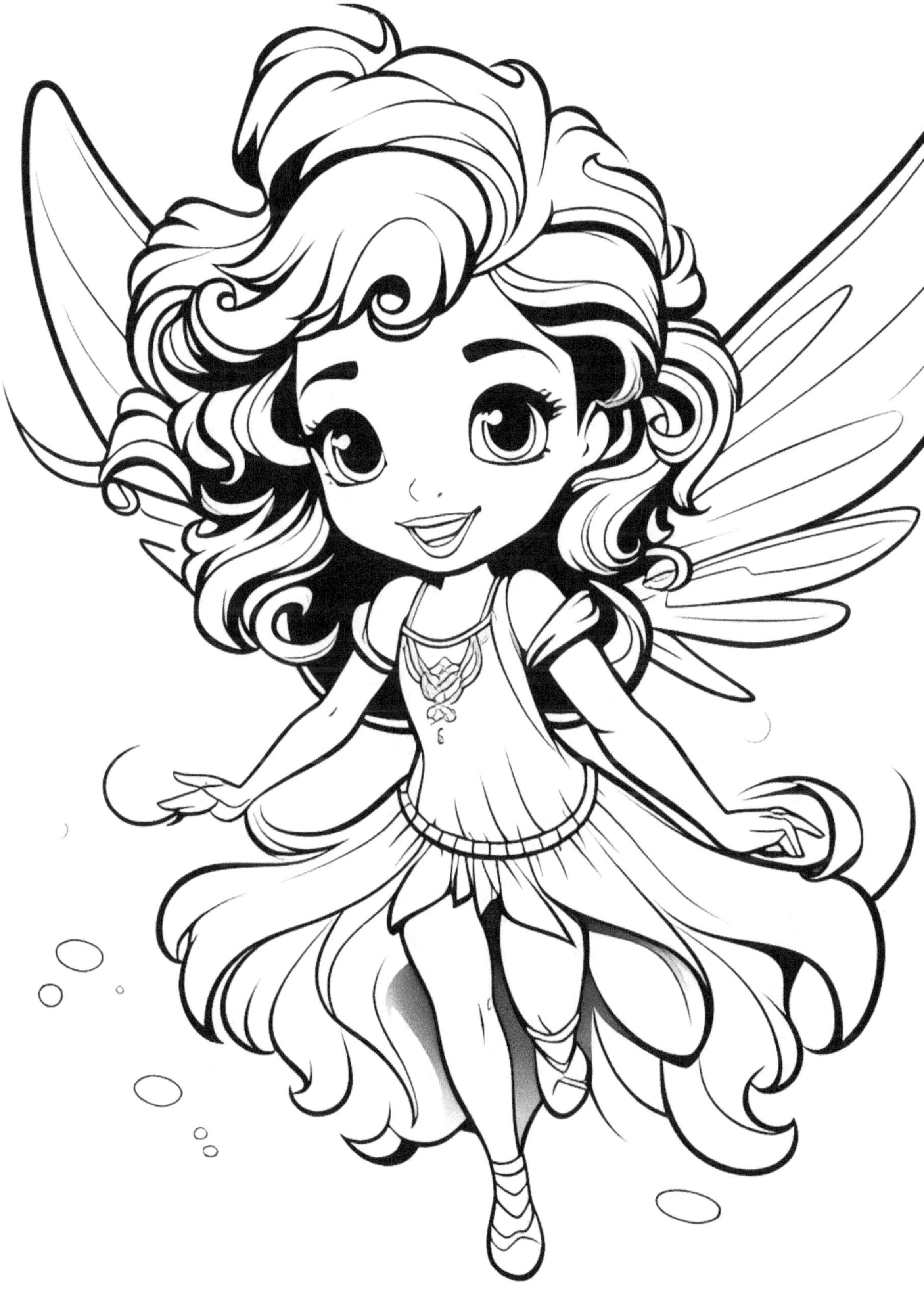

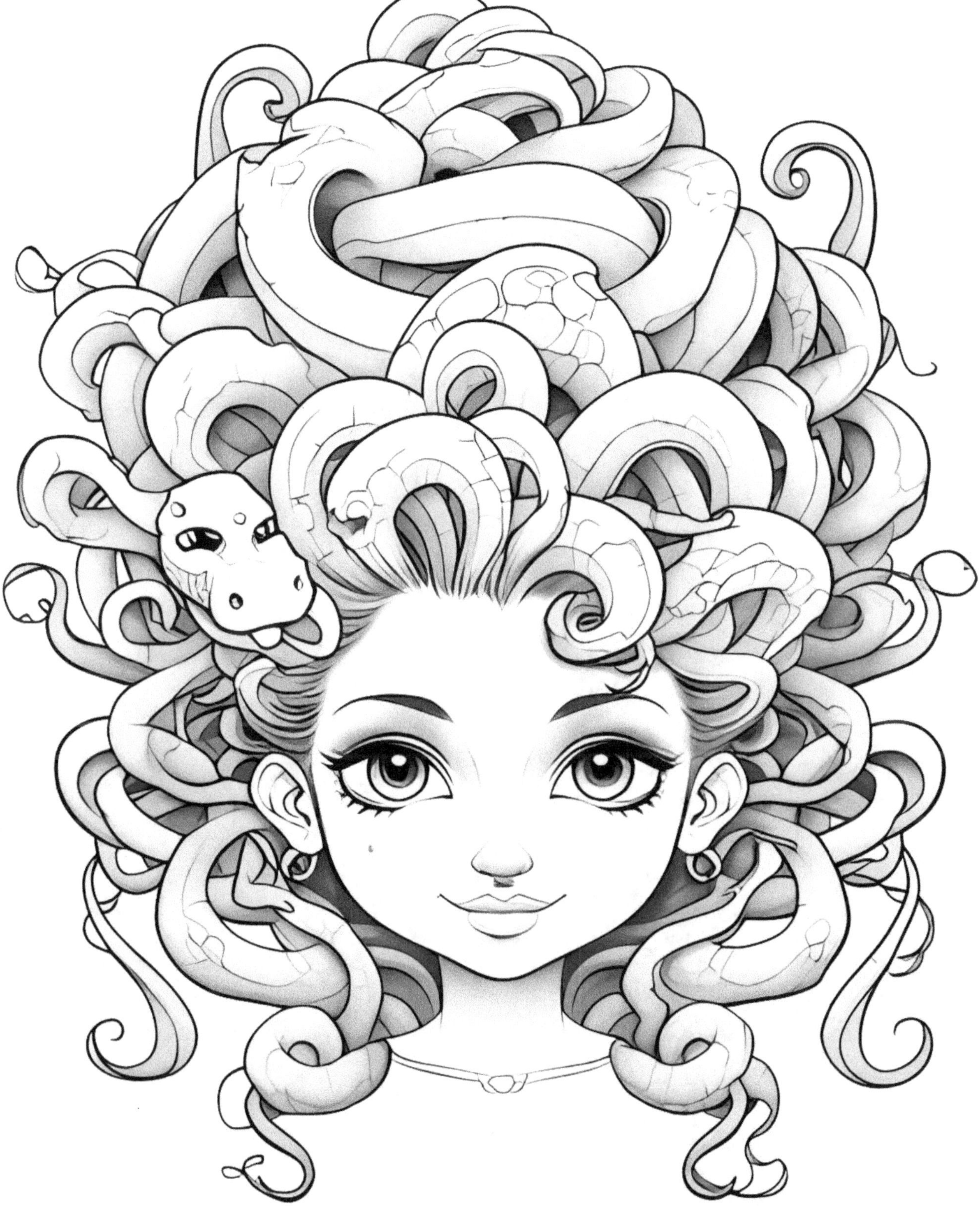

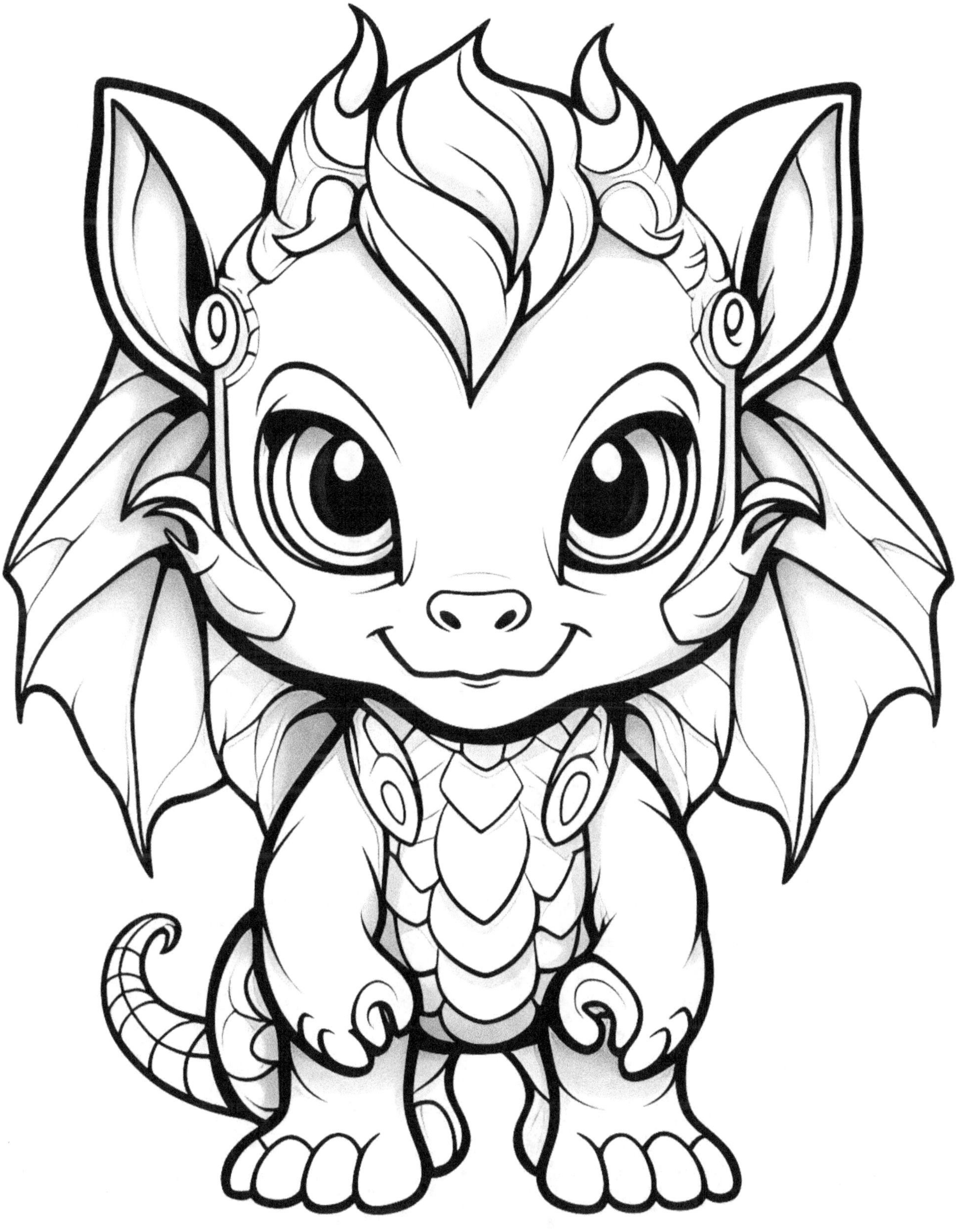

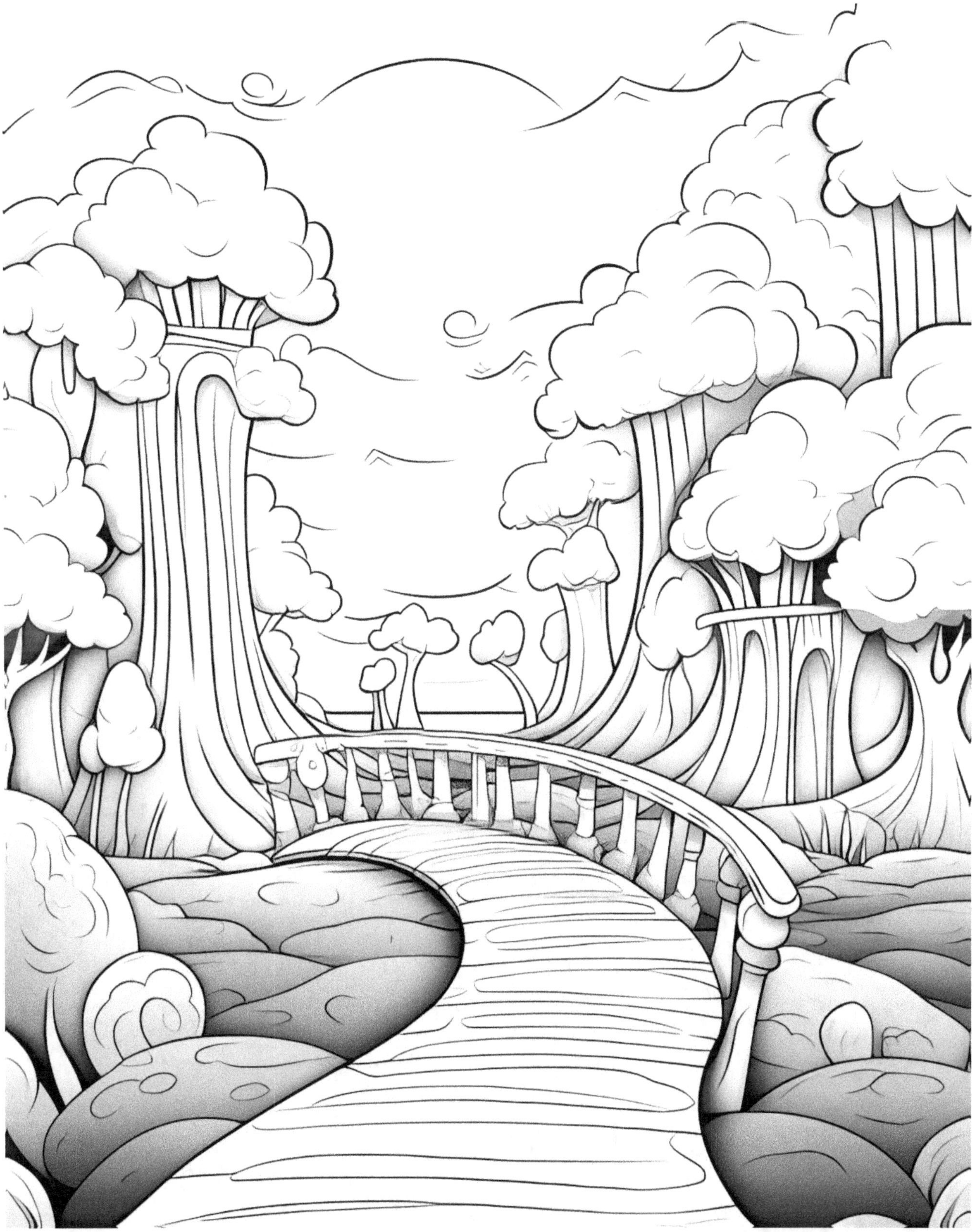

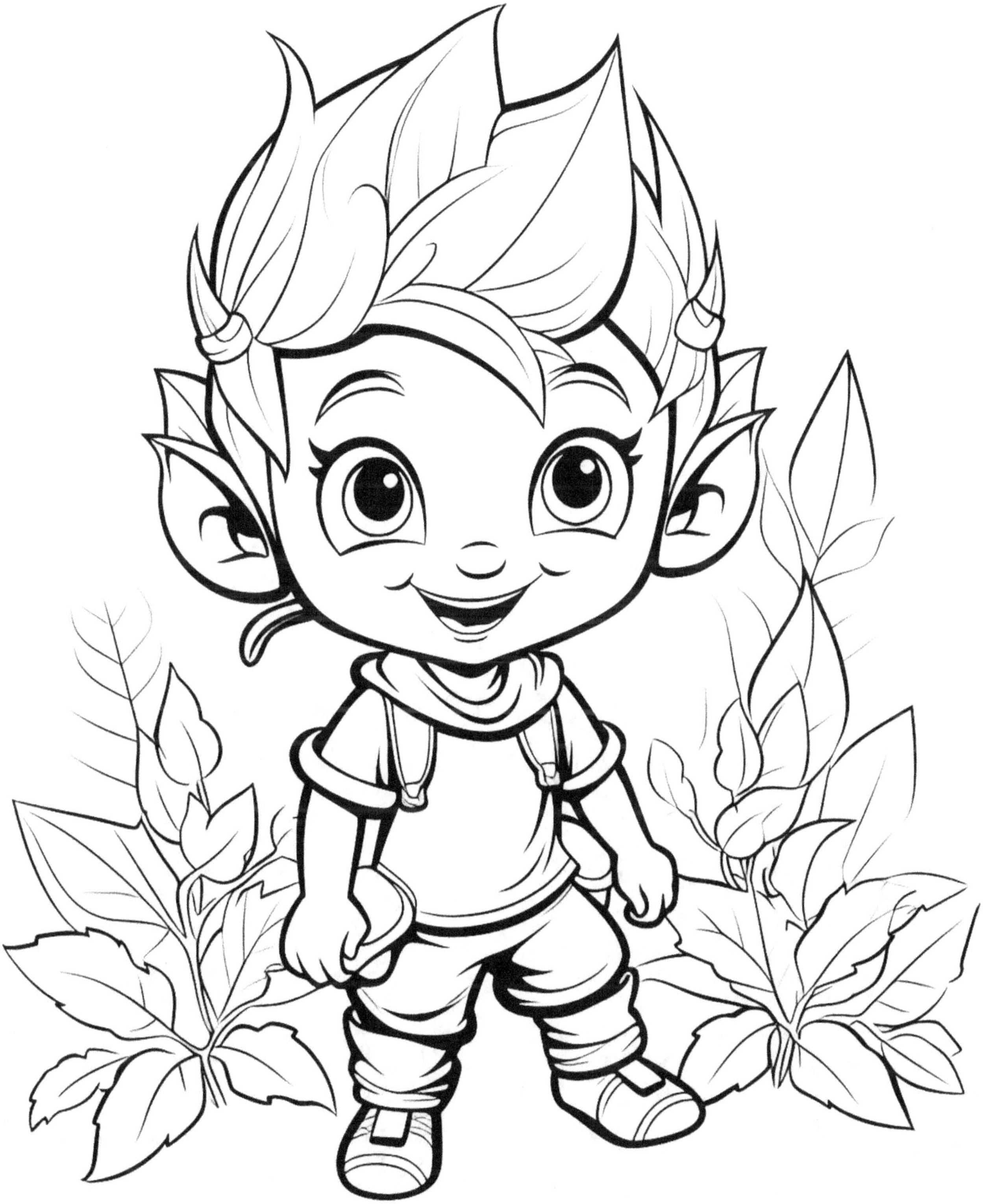

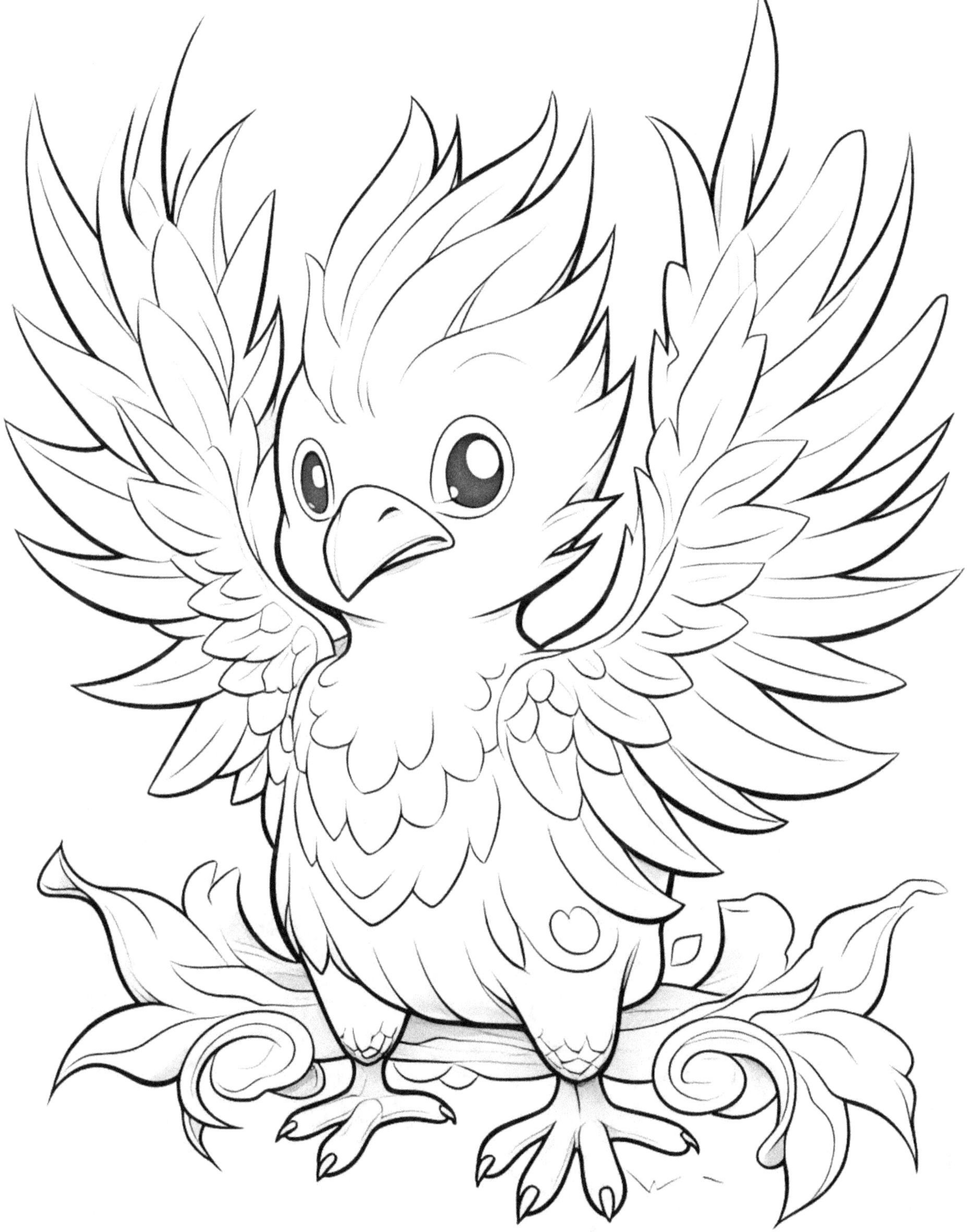

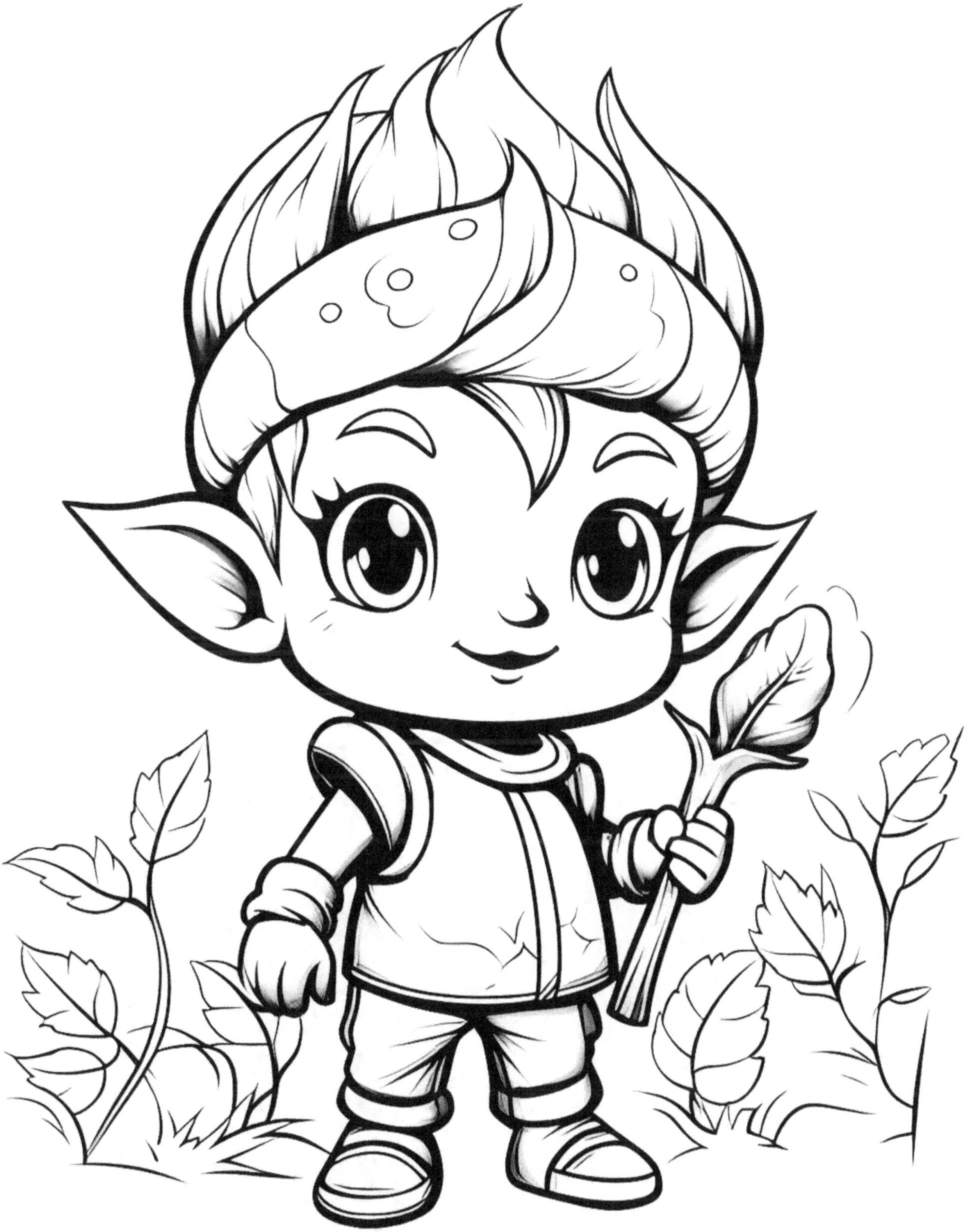

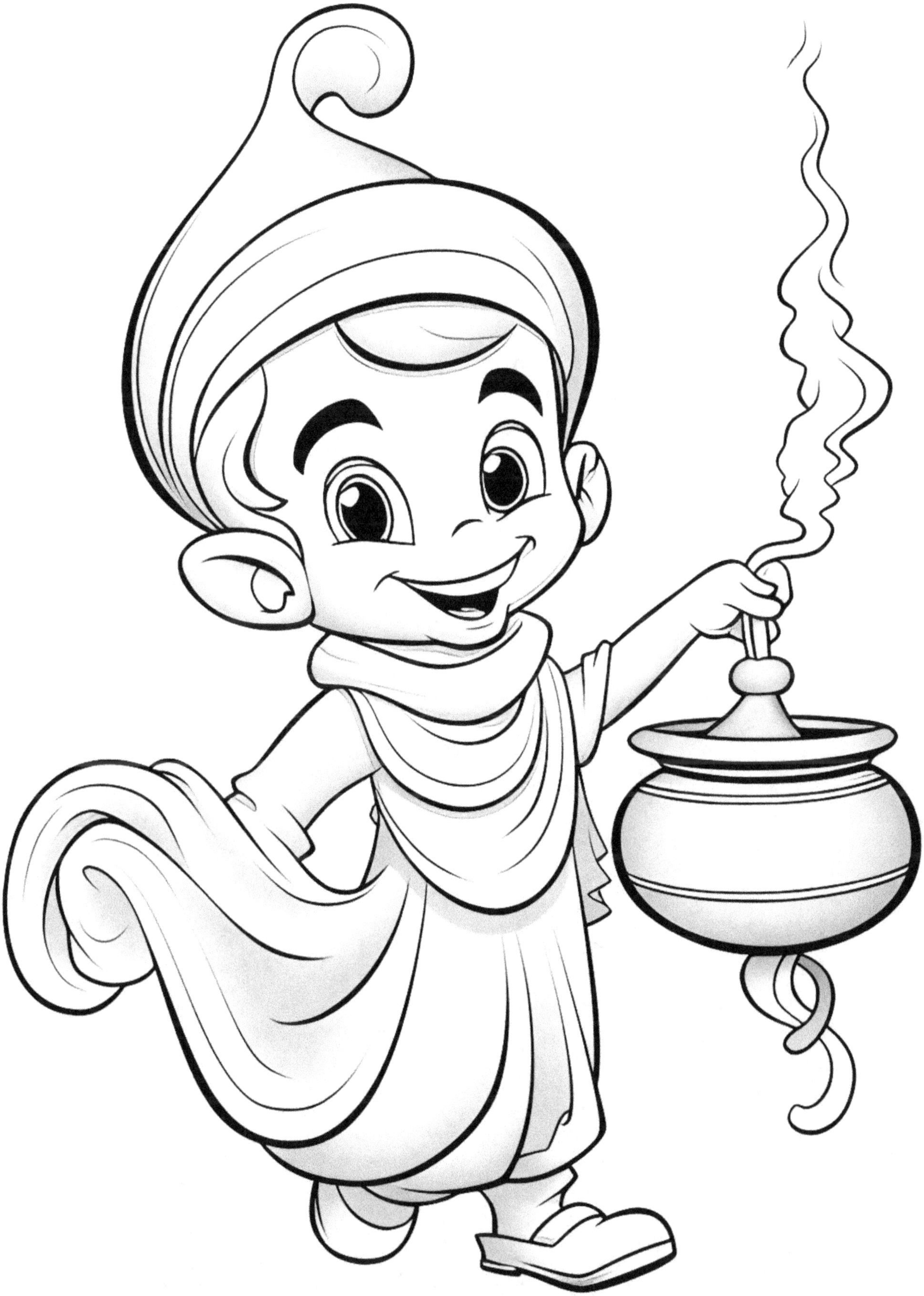

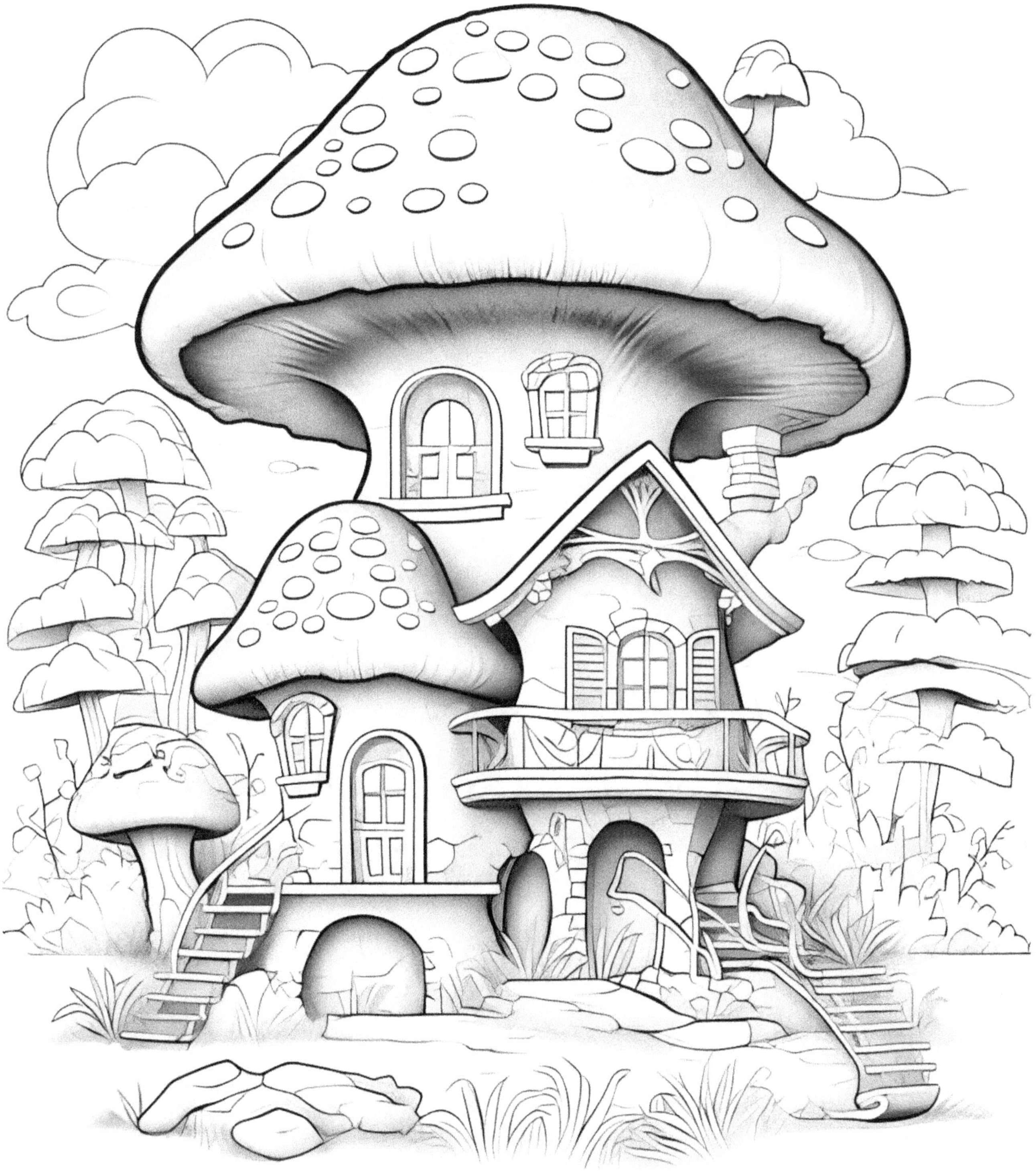

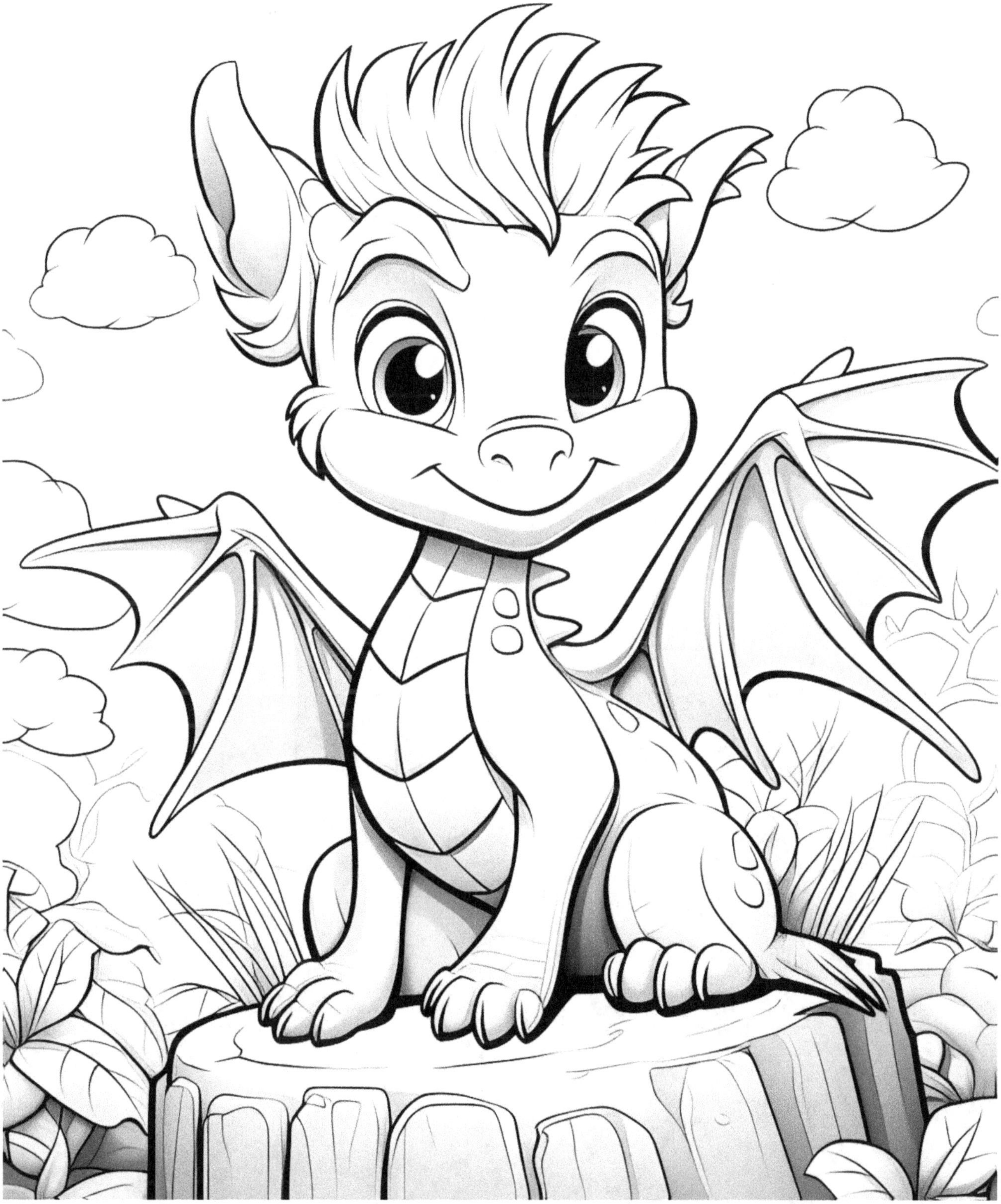

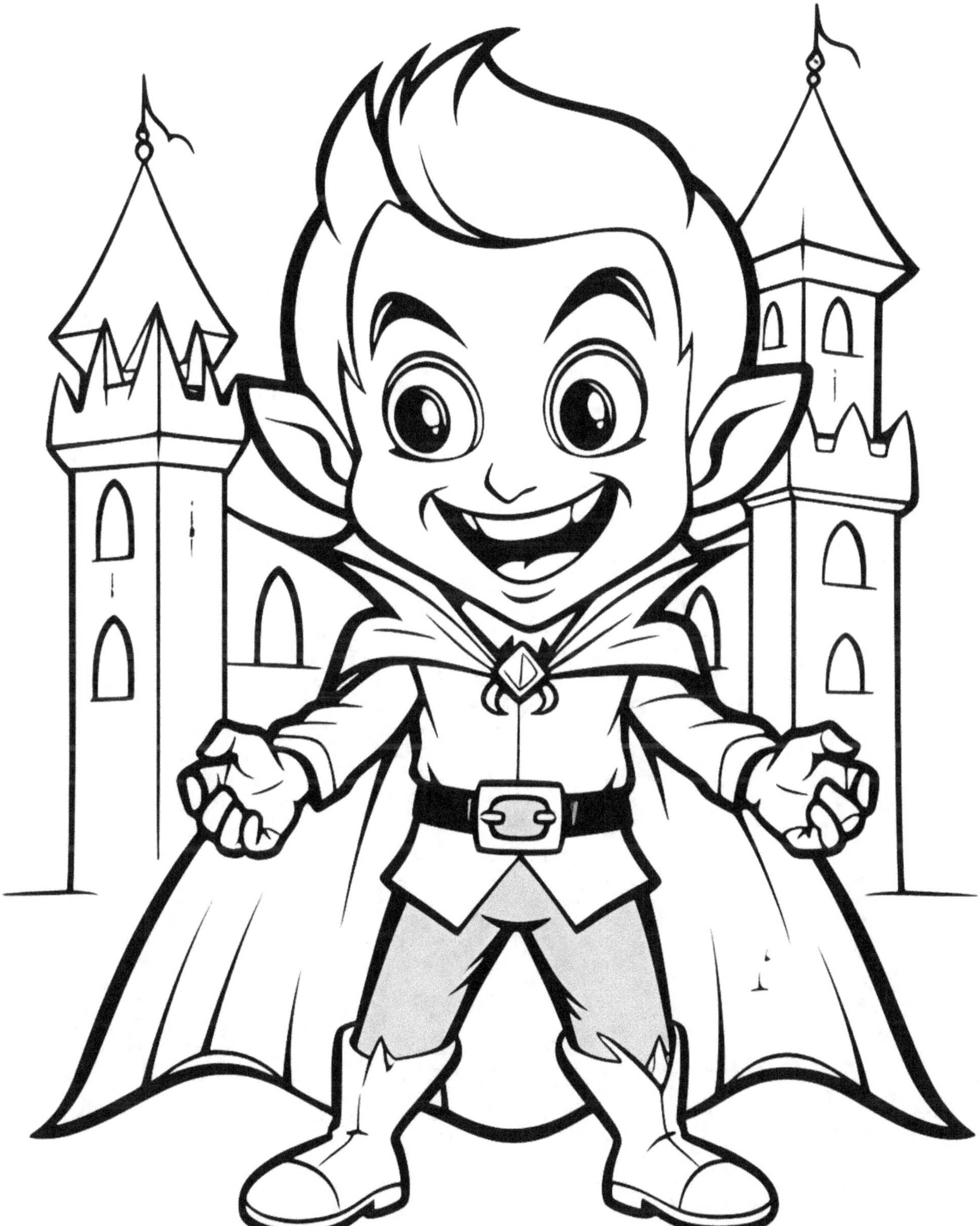

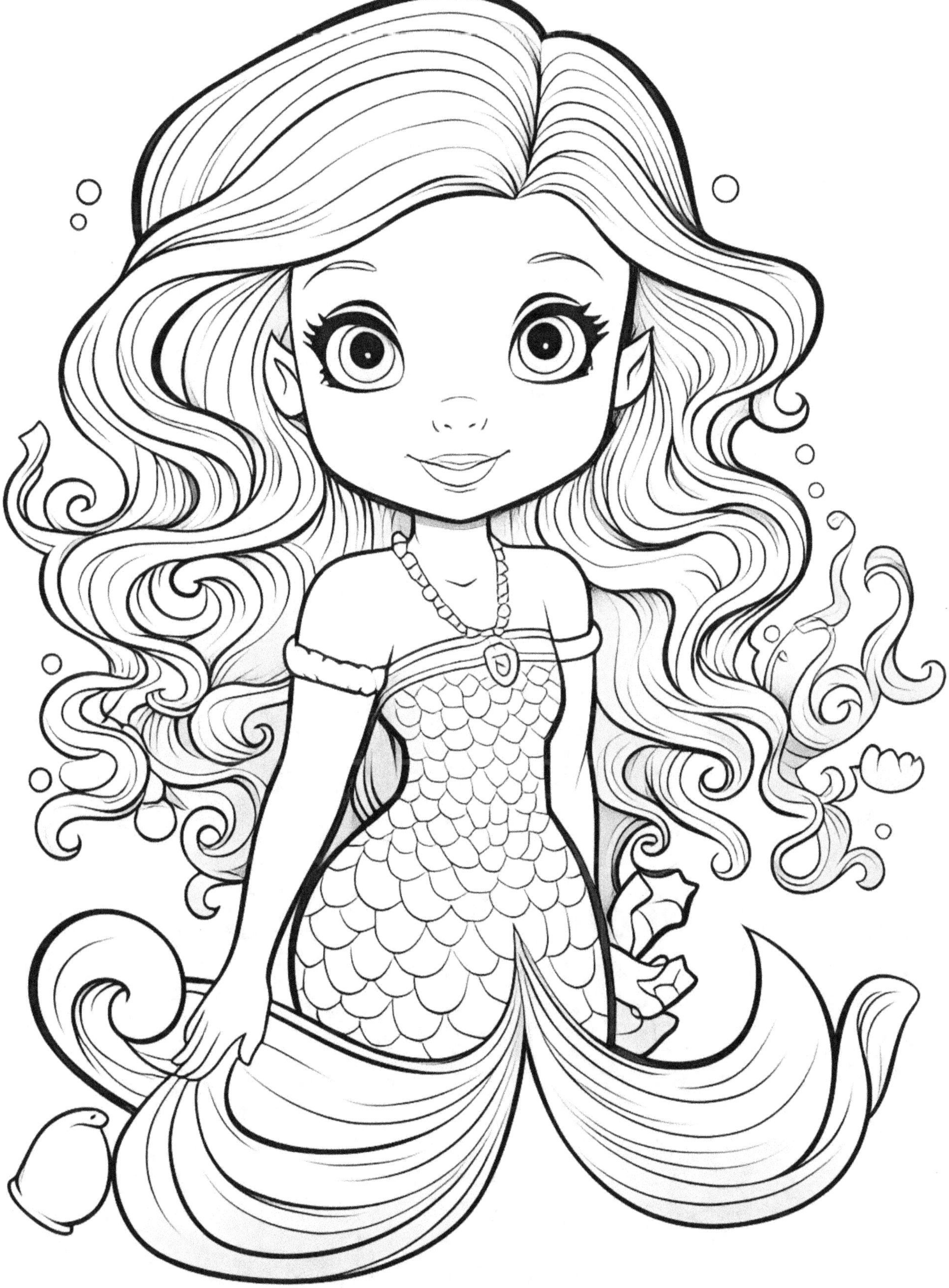

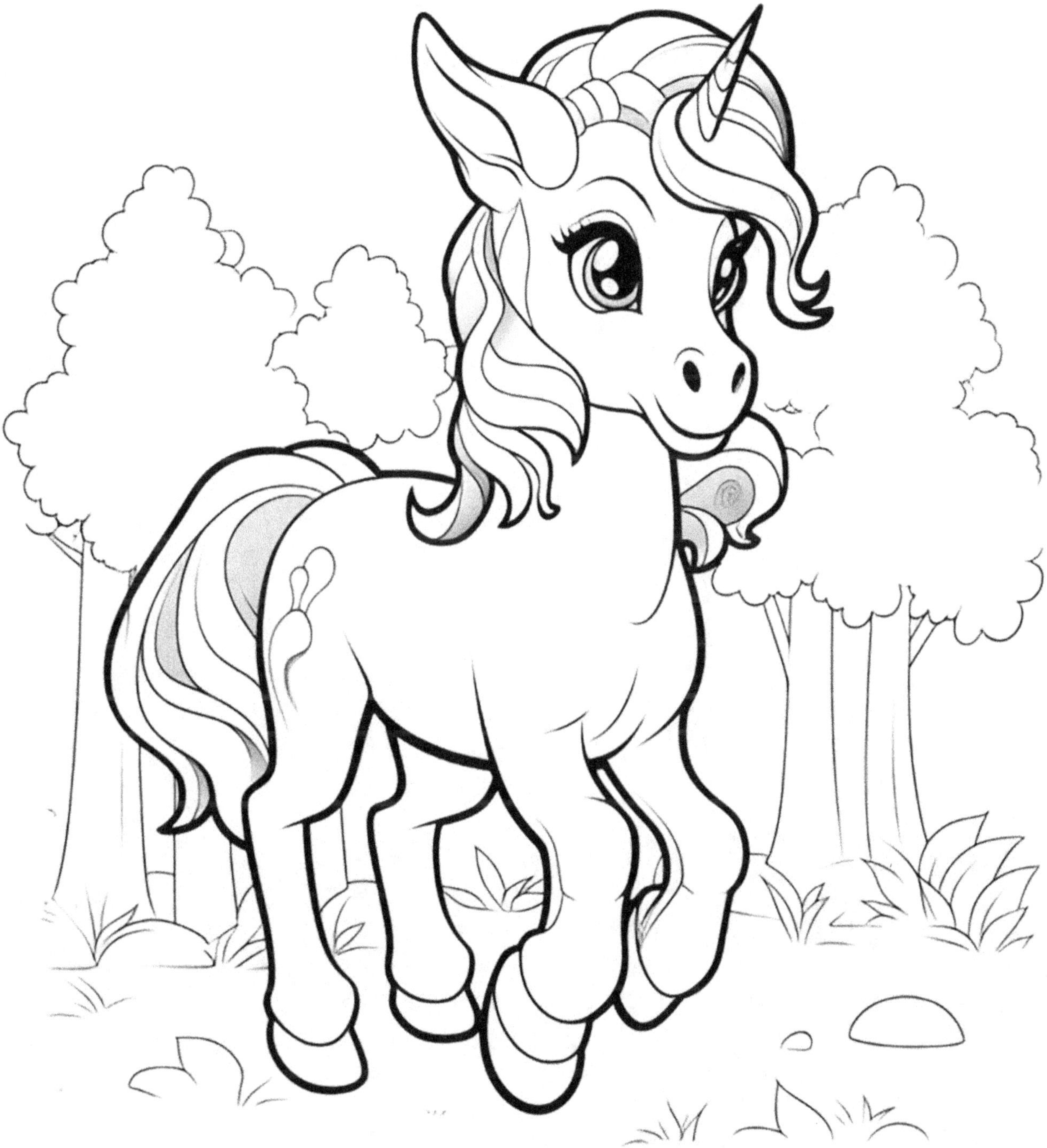

www.ingramcontent.com/pod-product-compliance
Lightning Source LLC
Chambersburg PA
CBHW082156290526
45794CB00008B/3324
* 9 7 9 8 8 6 1 5 3 2 4 9 5 *